The Stirling Bomber

John Reid

Stirling Mk.I N3641, built at Rochester, Kent in August 1940, was one of the first ten production models manufactured. Ordered under contract No.763825/36 N3641 was delivered to 7 Squadron on 12th August 1940 and given the code MG-D flying a total of four Ops. It was transferred to 26 Conversion Flight coded 'P' and then to 1651 Conversion Unit coded 'C'. It finally became a training aircraft and was renumbered 3010M in April 1942.

Text © John Reid, 2018.
First published in the United Kingdom, 2018,
by Stenlake Publishing Ltd.
Telephone: 01290 551122
www.stenlake.co.uk

Printed by
P2D, 1 Newlands Road, Westoning, MK45 5LD

ISBN 9781840338218

The publishers regret that they cannot supply copies of any pictures featured in this book.

Picture Acknowledgements

Bombardier (Short Bros) PLC: pages 1, 2, 3, 4, 5, 9, 19 (upper), 27, 29, 30, 31, 48
Jim Breeze: 21
Noel Chaffey: 26
Cherry Cherrington: 18 (both), 34
Bob Dalton: 33
Les Ede: 35
Roy Glass: 36
John Graf: inside back cover
Stan Jarvis: 40
Tom Knox: 17
Ernie Morehen: 13, 14
Eric Nicholson: 41

J. Reid Collection: 8, 1, 12, 47
Rolls Royce PLC Heritage Trust: 28
Lorna Russell: 43
Margaret Scott (née Sharrett): 22
Roy Scott: 24, 25, 45
Lance Smith Collection: 16, front cover
Rosemary Snowdon: 46
R. Spafford: 44
Roy Spear: 37, 38, 39
Arthur Stobbs: 42
Bob Todd: 32
Ian Tonkin: 23
Ted Wood: 19 (lower), 20

The S31/M4 half scale Stirling prototype made by Shorts to test the aircraft's aerodynamics. Built mainly of plywood it was powered by four 90hp Pobjoy engines. Testing was carried out at the RAF's Aeroplane and Armament Experimental Establishment (A&AEE) Martlesham Heath in Suffolk. From the results of the tests modifications were made to the undercarriage to assist in take-off and landing runs.

Introduction

Early in 1936 the Air Ministry prepared a specification B.12/36 for the design and production of a four engine bomber capable of using runways carrying a minimum 8,000lb bomb load 3,000 miles.

Altogether nineteen aviation companies were provided with the specification and of these five eventually tendered designs. Two companies, Supermarine Aviation based at Woolston, Southampton, and Shorts Bros of Rochester, Kent, began to prepare and build prototypes. However, the aircraft being constructed by Supermarine at Woolston, L6889 and L6890, were badly damaged in a German air raid on 26th September 1940 and the company withdrew from the project with all work abandoned. This left Shorts as the only remaining contractor with Sir Arthur Gouge as the chief designer and Claude Lipscombe as his assistant chief designer who continued with the work. Unlike Supermarine, instead of building a full scale prototype they chose to build a half scale flying prototype during 1938; this was intended to iron out any aerodynamic problems during the test flights. Fitted with four 90hp Pobjoy Niagara engines and built entirely of plywood the aircraft was given the designation S31 but subsequently became known as M4. Once constructed the M4 was first flown on 19th September 1938 by Short's chief test pilot John Lankester Parker and assisted by Hugh Gordon. Trials were carried out at the RAF'S Aeroplane and Armament Experimental Establishment Martlesham Heath, Suffolk and in only a few short weeks all the testing had been carried out with mostly satisfactory results. The most concern was expressed regarding the excessive take-off and landing runs. To overcome this problem it was suggested that the wing angle be increased from 3½ degrees to 6½ degrees. This posed a major complication as work on the design and production of tooling had been progressing and was well advanced thereby making such a huge modification impossible. The solution proposed by Shorts, which was accepted, was to add 3 degrees to the ground angle by adding extra height to an already elongated undercarriage. As a consequence of this adaptation the aircraft was to be plagued throughout its service life with problems due to its fragile and complex construction of the undercarriage. The modified undercarriage was fitted to the M4 together with more powerful 115hp Pobjoy Niagara Mk.IV engines and first flew 10th January 1939. At the same time as further testing was being carried out on the M4 prototype it had been decided to start production on two full scale prototypes officially designated Stirling MK.I/P1.

Almost immediately work began on the full scale prototypes Serials L7600 and L7605 the Air ministry ordered 100 production aircraft. L7600 was built at the Rochester factory and was fitted out with four Mk.I 1,150 hp Bristol Hercules engines and fully armed with three turrets comprising a Frazer Nash nose turret with two Browning .303 machine guns, a Frazer Nash tail turret with four Browning .303 machine guns and a Frazer Nash ventral turret armed with two Browning .303 machine guns, this turret being fully retractable into the fuselage.

The maiden flight of L7600 took place on 14th May 1939 but delays in receiving the Hercules Mk.III engines resulted in the aircraft remaining fitted with the inferior Hercules Mk.I. All went well with the take-off and following a short test flight upon touching down one of the brakes seized and one undercarriage collapsed rapidly followed by the other one causing the aircraft to skid on its belly for a considerable distance. The main cause of the failure was put down to the back arch of the unit being constructed from light alloy extrusions. This was modified on the second prototype using stronger steel tubing. L7600 was so badly damaged it was written off and scrapped. The accident put the whole project back by many weeks and meant some serious redevelopment and reinforcing of the undercarriage but after a huge effort by everyone at Shorts the second prototype L7605 was readied for its first flight which took place on 3rd December 1939 and was completely successful. The only procedure not carried out (on purpose) was a full retraction of the undercarriage which was kept in the down position during the short flight. Ground testing continued and the aircraft carried out its second full test flight on 24th December 1939. This again was completed without any problems with the undercarriage being fully retracted, all doors and controls functioning satisfactorily. Further flights were carried out and the test program continued without any further mishaps.

From the outset Shorts initial design for B.12/36 was for a 112ft wingspan along the lines of the Sunderland flying boat that was already in production. However, the Air Ministry decided to restrict this partly on available hanger size but mainly on the fact they feared the aircraft might become too large and unwieldy and require long runways plus there would be saving in construction time and materials. The final accepted wingspan was shortened to 99ft 1in with the aircraft to be powered by four Bristol Hercules 14 cylinder air cooled radial engines. The wings each contained seven fuel tanks with a total capacity of 2,254 gallons which apart from the leading edge (No7 tanks) were covered in Semape, a self-sealing rubber compound. Large wing flaps, designed by Arthur Gouge, were fitted to the wing trailing edge to reduce take-off and landing runs.

The fuselage was an all-metal construction in four major interchangeable sections with thought being given to the repair of any subsequent battle damage. This later proved to be of huge benefit. The underside of each section formed part of the bomb bays which were divided into three narrow cells. This construction was to limit the maximum size of any bombs carried, the largest being 2,000lbs. Various combinations, usually up to 14,000lbs of HC (High Capacity), MC (Medium Capacity), AP (Armour Piercing), GP (General Purpose) and SBCs (Small Bomb Containers) were carried depending on the type of target attacked and the distance involved. For example a maximum 14,000lb load would consist of 7 x 2,000lb AP and a 12,000lb load would be made up of 24 x 500lb or 6 x 1,000lb + 24 x 250lb GP bombs. If an all incendiary load was carried it would usually be made up of a combination of SBCs each typically containing 150 x 4lb incendiaries, up to 10 SBCs could be carried. The wing and fuselage dimensions were to remain virtually unchanged on all the Stirlings built but variations in construction were introduced as production continued throughout the war. These differences were mainly attributed to changes in the defensive armament fitted to the various marks with some minor internal modifications plus the fitting of more powerful engines as required. There were a total of seven variants in total produced from the prototypes to the final Mk.V transport version. The early aircraft MK.Is and MK.IIIs were built to carry bombs, mines and special SOE containers but in late 1943 the aircraft was taken off front line duties due to it being unable to reach a more practical bombing altitude. In view of this it was decided to further modify the fuselage and the Stirling was rated as the MK.IV and was adapted to carry up to 20 fully-equipped paratroopers or it was fitted with a glider towing bridle under the rear turret to enable Horsa or Hamilcar gliders loaded with either troops or jeeps and guns etc. and be towed to landing sites in occupied Europe. Some sea mining operations were carried on when the bombing sorties were stopped and many container supply runs were made to provision Resistance fighters with arms, ammunition, radio equipment and explosives. Other Mk.IIIs of 199 and 171 Squadrons were left in their original bomber configuration and slightly modified by being fitted with top secret Radio Counter Measure transmitters called Mandrel used to jam the German early warning radar. At the end of the war the Stirling once again went through a transformation to become the transport variant Mk.V. This was capable of carrying large loads of stores or was fitted with up to 20 passenger seats and became a virtual airliner in the late 1940s.

*** In line with decisions made during 1932 and 1939 it had been decided to give all RAF bombers names of British cities or towns. The first four engine heavy bomber produced for the RAF was named 'Stirling' after the Scottish town.

Stirling N3635. Rocket assisted take-off trials at Boscombe Down. A barrel shaped container holding twelve rockets was fixed under each wing and was progressively fired using a rheostat linked to the main throttles in the cockpit. On 16th August 1941 the aircraft swung violently to port due to the starboard rockets firing before those on the port side. The Stirling caught fire but the pilot F/Lt B. Huxtable was able to walk away unhurt. N3635 was officially written off 1st January 1942.

View across the vast production area of Short's factory in Rochester. This section was used to fit the gun turrets.

Main production line at Rochester, 31st Jan 1941. These are all early Mk.I models.

Crew of Stirling W7633 LS-P XV Squadron, Bourne. *Left to right*: Sgt F. Mitchell, W/Op; P/O Bill McAlpine; F/O Hal Miles, Pilot; WAAF Driver; F/Sgt Scotty Goodall, B/A; P/O Mac McCaffery; Sgt Bert Wright, A/G; Sgt Paul Curtis, A/G. The aircraft completed eight Ops with XV Squadron but following a wheels up landing returning from a raid on Genoa on 23rd October 1942 it was repaired and transferred to 1657 CU. On 18th March 1944 W7633 crashed at Little Thurlow three miles WNW of Stradishall killing all the crew except for the rear gunner Sgt J.H. Dacre who was dragged from his turret by a local lady, Enid Gridley, but died from his injuries on 4th April 1944.

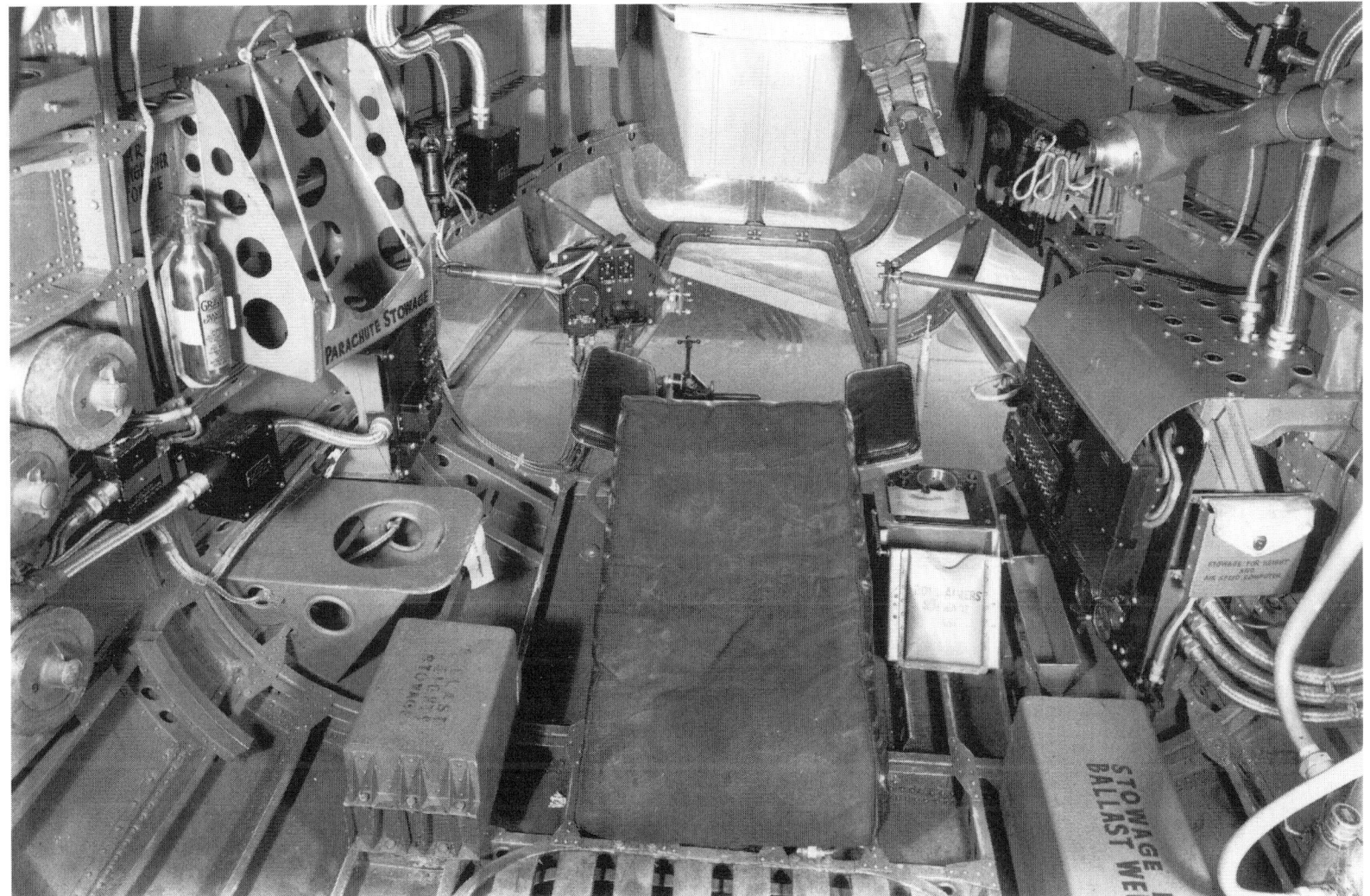

Bomb aimer's position. On the right-hand side are the bomb selector and sequencing units that enabled the correct dropping order of the bombs to maintain the aircraft's centre of gravity. Bombs could only be dropped when the bomb doors were fully open – the controls for these being on the right-hand side of the pilot's instrument panel. Provided the bomb selector switches were correctly engaged the bombs could be released by the pilot.

Bombing up with 500lb GP bombs and in the background the mobile bowser is topping up the fuel tanks with 2,300 gallons of high octane petrol. This photograph gives a good indication of the 22ft height of the cockpit from the ground. Ground crew could also walk safely under the propellers even with the engines running.

Line up of 75 Squadron aircrew taken at Newmarket May 1943. The aircraft is BK810 AA-G that was delivered to the Squadron on 24th April 1943. Various crews flew the Stirling on a total of thirteen bombing and mining ops from the 5th May to 22nd June 1943. When on a raid to Mulheim, Netherlands, it was shot down at 0210hrs by a combination of flak and night fighter flown by Hptmn Wilhelm Herget 1/NJG1, and crashed at Oostrum, Netherlands. Pilot P/O F.M McKenzie was killed together with Bomb Aimer F/Sgt J.F. Blank. The remaining five crew survived and were taken PoW.

Stirling Mk.III BK703 OJ-K 149 Squadron. Built by Austin Motors Ltd at Longbridge and delivered to XV Squadron on 2nd March 1943. However, the aircraft was almost immediately transferred to 149 Squadron on 10th March 1943. After completing 24 Ops the Stirling was shot down on a raid to Cologne 28th June 1943 by Lt Gunther Franz 5/NJG1. The Stirling crashed near a farm on the outskirts of Netersel, Netherlands, with loss of all the crew.

Engine fitters servicing the starboard inner Hercules XI engine of Stirling R9189 HA-K 218 Squadron Downham Market.

Stirling R9189 HA-K 218 Squadron, Downham Market. Taken on charge by 218 on 13th September 1942. The Stirling completed a total of 30 Ops with P/O M.W. Pettit at the controls on 20 of these sorties. On 28th February 1943 R9189, piloted by P/O E.B. Cozens, was taking off at 1815hrs for a raid on St. Nazaire when the aircraft swung violently to starboard and the undercarriage collapsed. There were no injuries to the crew but the damage to the fuselage was such it was considered un-repairable and was struck off charge 20th April 1943.

Crew of Stirling R9189 HA-K.

Loading sea mines Lakenheath 1943. The Stirling could carry a total of six mines and the one shown is a Mk.III 1,500lb of which 750lb of its total weight was high explosive. The mine could be dropped in enemy waters from heights ranging from a few hundred feet up to 15,000ft. Most of the instant triggering mechanisms were magnetic or acoustic although some mines could lie dormant for several days allowing shipping to pass over unharmed giving the enemy a false sense of security and the minesweepers in chaotic uncertainty.

North Creake 1944. The crew shown here were originally attached to 199 Squadron but when 171 Squadron was formed from 199 'C' Flight on 8th September 1944 this crew was subsequently reassigned to 171. *Standing left to right*: F/O Doug Halliwell, Special Wireless Operator; P/O A. (Jack) Tipple, Navigator; Sgt E. (Nobby) Clarke, Rear Gunner; F/Lt Hugh Coventry, Pilot, RAAF; F/Sgt B. (Tom) Knox, Flight Engineer, RAAF; P/O Mike Scottie, Mid Upper Gunner. *Kneeling*: W/O C. (Dave) Skewes, Wireless Operator, RAAF; F/O N.P. (Fred) Beatty, Bomb Aimer, RCAF. F/O Halliwell went on to become the Squadron Signals Leader.

Stirling Mk.IV LJ612 E7-L. 570 Squadron at dispersal, Rivenhall, Essex. The aircraft is being readied for an SOE Op to drop supplies to Resistance fighters in occupied Europe. Full containers are on the ground under the nose and at the rear door wicker panniers are being unloaded from a lorry. The nose art is shown enlarged in the next photograph

Nose art Stirling LJ612 E7-L illustrated by a cartoon of a chipmunk holding a bomb with "L's A Comin" written above. The 'mission log' shows that at the time the photograph was taken LJ612 had completed 22 sorties comprising eighteen SOE (Special Operations Executive), one Bombing Op, two Glider Tows and one Air Sea Rescue Search. Regular pilot F/O R.E. Davison at the controls.

Stirling Mk.III EF427 LS-A. XV Squadron. Mildenhall, *circa* June 1943. EF427 was delivered to XV Squadron on 30th May 1943 and flown on each of its seven operational sorties by P/O G.G. Judd. On 30th July 1943 EF427 and her crew were assigned a target in Remscheid, a town located in the extremely heavily defended area known as the Ruhr, and took off from Mildenhall at 2242 hrs. Arriving over the target at approximately 0115 hrs the aircraft was coned by searchlights and sustained several hits by flak including a direct hit in the forward cockpit area. EF427 crashed in a field near the main Manheim–Bergan road with four of the crew including the pilot P/O Judd being killed. Three crew survived and were taken PoW.

A rare flying shot of Stirling Mk.IV LJ977 V8-B 570 Squadron. Flown by the Squadron's Commanding Officer W/Cdr R.J.M. Bangay DFC LJ977 is homeward bound from the first glider tow to Arnhem on 17th September 1944. This was part of the 'Market Garden' operation to secure the bridge over the River Rhine. Photo taken from S/Ldr Hudson's Stirling over the North Sea. The aircraft carried the nose art "Beer is Best" depicting a beer barrel with wings. LJ977 was delivered to 570 Sqd coded V8-M on 18th August 1944 and flew ten Ops. To 295 Squadron on 10th December 1944 coded 8Z-G – no Ops flown. Then transferred to 620 Squadron 8th February 1945 flying two more Ops and finally to 196 Squadron 14th June 1945. Struck off charge 5th June 1947.

Stirling Mk.IV LJ977 V8-B towing Horsa Glider on the first day of the Arnhem 'Market Garden' drop 17th September 1944. The aircraft was flown by W/Cdr Bangay DFC together with Squadron Ops Officer F/Lt Ted (Timber) Wood as Bomb Aimer. They both completed 'D' Day, Arnhem and the Rhine Crossing towing gliders and on each occasion they had the same glider pilot – Captain, later Major, Hugh Bartlett of the Glider Pilot Regiment. Major Bartlett would have been at the controls of the Horsa Glider when this photograph was taken.

Stirling Mk.IV LK119 NF-R 138 Squadron (Special Duties) Tempsford, Beds, January 1945. LK119 completed 29 SOE Ops with 138 Squadron and on 20th March 1944 was transferred to 161 Squadron coded MA-Y, flying a further five Ops. On 30th March 1944 the aircraft and crew took off from Tempsford at 2103 hrs on SOE Op Bit 14 the destination DZ (Drop Zone) given as No.244 Grollvann 13km SW of Lyngdal, Norway. The Stirling was attacked by a night fighter from Kjevik and exploded in the air with remains falling in thick forest at Andsmyra near Hegland, Holt. All the crew were killed and initially buried near the crash site but after the war was over they were laid to rest in the cemetery at Arendal, Aust-Agder, Norway. Crew: F/Lt E.F.C. Kidd, Pilot; Sgt R.A. Burgess, F/Eng; F/Sgt G.A. Heath, Nav; F/O T. McCauley, B/A; F/Sgt H. Minshull, A/G Dispatcher; F/Sgt A.D. Shopland, A/G; W/O A.M. Taylor, W/Op.

RAF Rivenhall, Flying Control Staff: S/Ldr P.G. Antrobus, 3rd from right middle row; LACW Margaret Sharrett, 4th from right middle row; LACW Jane Sharpe, 5th from right middle row; F/Sgt Mac Vicar Pollock, 2nd from left front row; Sgt Marjorie Young, 1st from left front row; F/Sgt Herbert A/G, 2nd from right middle row.

Sergeant Len Tonkin, Pilot, RAAF. He is seen alighting from Stirling R9326 BU-G 214 Squadron based at Stradishall. The date was 30th May 1942 and the photograph was taken on return from the first 1,000 bomber raid on Cologne codename 'Operation Millennium'. He is carrying a Thermos vacuum flask and an Irvin Observers type parachute pack. Detailed for a raid on Essen 1st June 1942 Sgt Tonkin was forced to return early after two hours due to a burst supply line in the rear turret. R9326 was flown on the following two Ops to Emden and a mining sortie off the Frisian Islands by P/O Massie and on 11th June 1942 Sgt Tonkin was assigned the same target area loaded with four mines. The Stirling was coned near the target by several searchlights and trying to fly under them it crashed on the uninhabited island of Memmert, off the coast of Germany. All eight members of the crew survived and were picked up by the Germans and taken PoW.

295 Squadron Stirling Mk.IV 8E-U being serviced at Rivenhall, Essex 1945. Due to the height of the aircraft a large assortment of scaffolding was required to reach the engines and cockpit area as can be seen from this photograph. Almost all the normal routine maintenance work was carried out in the open and the fitters even managed complete engine changes. Only major repairs were allocated hangar time.

Line up of 295 and 570 Squadron Mk.IV Stirlings Rivenhall 1945. Starting from the nearest aircraft it has been possible to identify all the code letters as follows. E7-Q. 570 Squadron 'B' Flight; 8E-X. 295 Squadron 'B' Flight; 8E-K. 295 Squadron 'B' Flight; 8E-W. 295 Squadron 'B' Flight; V8-O. 570 Squadron 'A' Flight.

Stirling LJ899 QS-O 620 Squadron, Fairford, Gloucestershire. F/O P.S. Deacon and crew. Taken on charge by 620 Sqd on 25th February 1944 coded QS-O LJ889 flew a total of 30 Ops and a further two Ops with 190 Squadron after being transferred on 10th May 1945. F/O Deacon and this crew flew two Ops on this aircraft the first on 2nd Augusut 1944 "Frederick 16", France which was successful and then on 30th March 1945 they carried out "Crupper 23" to Norway. By now the code of the Stirling had been changed to D4-O. On 10th May 1945, while serving with 190 Squadron LJ899 coded L9-Z flown by F/O E. Atkinson was detailed to transport eighteen troops of the 1st Airborne Division to Gardermoen, Norway. Approaching Rjdafoss Lake near Torsby, Sweden the aircraft went out of control and crashed 0720 hrs at the water's edge of the lake. Of the crew only F/Sgt W.S. Long B/A was injured and taken to Middle Shole Hospital, Oslo. Four of the soldiers were killed and are buried in Kviberg nr Gothenburg. The other fourteen passengers escaped unhurt.

Stirling Mk.III BF509. Served with 149 Squadron and 1653 Conversion Unit. While with 149 Squadron it carried at various times the code letters OJ-N, OJ-B and OJ-R and completed a total of 29 Ops. While with 1653 CU it was coded E. This is an interesting photograph as it is evidently showing a pre-delivery test flight after leaving the Short & Harland Ltd factory where it was built. The Stirling has no codes and the turrets have no armaments fitted.

Stirling Mk. I. Series I. W7436 MG-D, 7 Squadron, Oakington. Built by Austin Motors Ltd. at the Longbridge factory, Birmingham. Delivered to 7 Squadron based at Oakington on 23rd July 1941. The Stirling completed a total of 24 Ops until 18th December 1941 when S/Ldr L.W.V. Jennens and his crew were detailed for a raid on Brest. The Stirling took off from Oakington on a daylight raid at 0948 hrs and was on track to the target when just off the Brittany coast it was attacked by several Me 109's. With the Stirling on fire S/Ldr Jennens attempted to formate on two other aircraft, no doubt for mutual protection, but was forced to turn towards the French coast. Two of the crew baled out but were too low and both were killed and the aircraft force landed in the sea near Plouguemeau, Finistere. The remaining five crew were captured and taken PoW. The airmen who died are buried in Plouguemeau Communal Cemetery.

Flight engineer's station. Equipped with a large panel of gauges, switches and valves the flight engineer was able to monitor the four Hercules engines and control the flow of fuel from the seven tanks contained in each wing.

Above: Wireless operator's station. One of a series of photographs produced by Shorts showing the interior 'working' compartments within the Stirling fuselage. Having closely examined this particular photograph it would appear to be fitted with equipment dating to the late 1930s/early 1940 and shown here is the R1082 receiver and T1083 transmitter sets. Later, when they became available, all heavy bombers including the Stirling that had a wireless operator in the crew were usually fitted out with the more powerful T1154 transmitter and a R1155 receiver, both large bulky items that are not present in this photograph. The installation shown here was fitted to early Mk's of the Stirling including the prototypes.

Facing page: Cockpit layout of early Hercules Mk.II powered aircraft. In the centre of the photograph are the 'Exactor' engine throttle control levers and below them the fuel mixture controls. In service this equipment was a source of persistent problems and complaints from aircrew were many. As the throttles were hydraulically operated they tended to 'lag' in operation and would not respond quickly enough. Constant priming was necessary to keep air out of the system and the levers were quite stiff to move. To get over the last problem the transmitters and receivers were removed and the glands eased off to bring the operating load down to an acceptable level. Many modifications were carried out to the throttle linkages but problems existed throughout the time the Stirling was operational.

EF411 OJ-K "King" 149 Squadron, Lakenheath, 1943. A Top Scorer. Delivered to 149 Squadron 21st June 1943 this aircraft went on to complete 69 operational sorties over enemy territory. Initially EF411 was coded OJ-M and was flown on its first operation to Mulheim on 22nd June 1943 by Sgt B.A. North. Sgt North flew EF411 as his personal aircraft for eighteen consecutive Ops and by the time he was assigned to his final target at Hanover on 27th September 1943 he had been promoted to Pilot Officer. Following this the aircraft was flown by a number of other pilots on a more random basis although some did fly several Ops consecutively. As this is one of the highest counts achieved by a front line bomber it is worth listing the Ops flown. Names of pilots involved: W/Cdr A. Elliot: one Op; F/Sgt W. Adams: two Ops; P/O R. Gill: one Op; F/Sgt R.N. Johnstone: one Op; F/Sgt T.C. Danvers: three Ops; Sgt M. Burdett: one Op; Sgt D.H. Hardwick: one Op; F/Sgt S.W. Holder: two Ops; F/Sgt R.W. Chapell: one Op; F/Sgt T.H. Strong: one Op; P/O R.E. Mackett: four Ops; Sgt R. Coates: two Ops; F/Sgt W.N. Smaill: one Op; F/Sgt J.H. Berry: ten Ops; F/Sgt H.N. Coventry: one Op; F/Sgt W.H. Mayo: two Ops; F/Lt R.J. Freeman: one Op; Sgt R.L. Todd: nine Ops; F/O A.R. Smith: four Ops; F/Sgt W.A. Phillips: one Op; F/Sgt K. Goldie: three Ops; F/O J.J. McKee: one Op; F/O R.E. Redman: one Op. On 2nd June 1941 the Squadron code for EF411 was changed to OJ-K. The last operation which was on 24th August 1944 was an ASR for a ditched Stirling and the code was changed to OJ-Y. The Stirling was transferred to 1653 CU on 29th August 1944 for training purposes and it survived the war and was struck off charge 24th April 1945.

LK171 "WES" "Shooting Stars" 295 Squadron, Harwell 1944. The crew names are painted on the nose of this Mk.IV Stirling and are as follows: Grp/Capt W.E. Surplice, DSO DFC Pilot; S/Ldr K.J. Bolton, Nav; P/O F.R. Morrow, B/A; P/O W.F. Wesley, F/Eng; P/O R.L. Chapin, A/G; W/O R. Dalton, W/Op. This Stirling did not carry the normal squadron code 8E or 8Z with an individual letter to follow, instead and something not usually found on a bomber it carried the initials of Group Captain W.E. Surplice "WES" who was the station commander at Harwell. On 2nd November 1944 LK171 failed to return from operation 'Halter 6' a supply drop for the Milorg Resistance Fighters in Norway. The crew had started to experience icing on the wings and engine intakes soon after crossing the Norwegian coast and when they arrived over the DZ 120 miles east of Oslo conditions were extremely bad. No reception lights could be seen and Surplice decided to abort the drop. He tried to gain height to get above the bad weather but ran into heavy snow and the situation went from bad to worse. As they were surrounded by mountains he gave the order to bale out and all the crew took to their parachutes and landed safely. Some were captured and taken PoW and others evaded and got back to England. Group Captain W.E. Surplice DSO DFC was killed when the aircraft crashed at Skarfjell near Vinklevaan. He was found still at the controls of his Stirling having given his life to enable his crew to escape.

General Eisenhower arriving by Dakota at Harwell on 22nd April 1944. He is accompanied by Air Commodore Hollinghurst, Sir Trafford Leigh-Mallory and Group Captain W.E. Surplice, Commanding Officer of Harwell home of 295 and 570 Squadrons. Seven months after this photograph was taken G/Cpt Surplice was killed on 2nd November 1944 when his Stirling LK171 crashed in Norway while on an SOE supply drop.

299 Squadron crew, Keevil, Wiltshire, 1944: Sgt H. Baker, RAF, F/Eng; W/O R. Ramsdon, RCAF, W/Op; F/O M. Farrell, RCAF, Pilot; P/O L. Ede, RAAF, Nav; F/Sgt J. Boa, RAF, B/A. The members of this crew took part in two glider tows and two re-supply drops to Arnhem (Market Garden) flying Stirling LK135 X9-U. The first Horsa tow carried nine troops, one small car, three motorcycles and four bicycles. The second Horsa tow delivered seven troops and two jeeps. The remaining two trips were to drop 24 containers and four panniers on each occasion.

A rare and unusual photograph taken during a training flight by a 1665 HCU Stirling. Both starboard engines have been shut down and the props feathered.

1657 Conversion Unit, Pilot Instructors, Stradishall, 25th September 1943: S/Ldr Roy Spear, RNZAF; F/Lt Corder; F/Sgt Henderson. Ground Staff: F/Lt Lamason; F/O Thompson.

An interesting study of a formation of Flying Fortresses of the 349th Bomb Squadron, 100th Bomb Group (The Bloody Hundredth) USAAF. This is one of several photographs taken by S/Ldr Roy Spear while on a test flight over Norfolk flying LK506 AK-S 1657CU. He had observed the Fortresses forming up for a daylight raid on Germany so he flew alongside for a while taking snaps and then realised that the American pilots had very carefully boxed him inside the formation. There was no escape and he had to continue towards the coast with the prospect of accompanying the Fortresses to Germany. The crew became rather concerned at what was going on as they were not wearing their warm combat clothing nor was the Stirling prepared for a long flight. It eventually all turned out okay as approaching the coast the American aircraft opened up the formation and the Stirling was able to slide out and return to base at Stradishall. It seems that the Americans were just having a bit of fun with Roy and his crew but they were not to know this until after they were allowed to leave the tight formation. The prospect of being the first and possibly the last Stirling to operate over Germany in broad daylight certainly did not appeal to the crew.

Stirling Mk.I R9192. 1657 CU. The Stirling was flying a Bullseye training flight that would closely resemble an operational bombing sortie. Approx 2045 hrs 30 miles west of Stradishall R9192 collided at 2,000ft with Wellington X3637 from 27 OTU. The photograph shows the extensive damage to the front turret and fuselage. The crew were on their final assessment before leaving Stradishall but they were able to return to base and land at 2110 hrs. Also on board were two army sergeants who were assessing the effects of the searchlight batteries on the ground, they beat a hasty retreat to their own camp not long after landing. The crew of the Wellington were all killed.

Stirling Mk.I EF390 MG-T. 7 Squadron based at Oakington but this photograph was taken at Witchford, May 1943. *Front row*: F/O R.H. Angus, Pilot, 2nd from left; Sgt Stan Jarvis, Flight Engineer, 5th from left. The normal crew for this aircraft were: F/O R.H. Angus, Pilot; F/O T.W. Boyd, Nav; Sgt W. Hawkins, W/Op; Sgt S. Jarvis, F/Eng; Sgt R.L. Clenahan, A/G; F/Sgt R.B. Smith, MU; Sgt D. McHaffie, R/G. Shortly after this photo was taken F/O Angus and American attached to the RAF joined the US 8th Air Force. This Stirling had a picture of Tommy Trinder the comedian painted on the nose. His catchphrase at the time was "You Lucky People". It was transferred to 214 Squadron 1st August 1943 coded BU-A and was shot down on a raid to Turin 12th August 1943 with the loss of all the crew.

Special Signals Technicians 199 and 171 Squadrons North Creake June 1944. All those present were directly responsible for the Top Secret 'Mandrel' radar jamming equipment carried in the Squadron's RCM aircraft. *Back Row*: LAC Dick Masters; A/C Bosworth; LAC Aldworth; LAC Ivor Burch; LAC Mike Connolly; A/C 'Dicky' Bird; LAC Dunthorn; LAC Breed. *Centre Row*: LAC George Reed; Cpl E. Nicholas; Cpl Joe Roe; Sgt M. Major; Cpl Len Boxell; LACW Yvonne ?; Cpl Light. *Front Row*: Cpl Mason; Cpl Wyatt; LAC Cosgrove; LAC Pete Ballard; LAC Terry Buckley; LAC Freddie White; LAC Tutt.

Air and ground crews sitting on a bomb trolley beside early Mk.I Stirling N3669, LS-H. XV Squadron Bourn 11th October 1942. N3669 was the 34th aircraft off the production line at Shorts, Rochester & Bedford Ltd factory. Delivered to 7 Squadron on 25th August 1941 coded MG-E and forming part of the first four engine heavy bomber squadron within the RAF. Having flown 20 Ops it was relocated to 26 Conversion Flight at Waterbeach 31st December 1941 and then to XV Squadron 16th May 1942 coded LS-C, LS-H, LS-A completing a further 47 Ops. Finally transferred to No.1 Air Armament Scholl in February 1943 it was re-numbered M3637.

Stirling EJ108 75 Squadron, Mepal, 1943. Crew standing on port stabiliser a few days before it was attacked and damaged on 4th November 1943 by a night fighter while on a mining Op in the Kattegat. The Stirling was returning early due to bad weather and 10/10 cloud. At map reference 5748N 0948E the night fighter approached from astern and raked the Stirling, hitting the rear turret and killing the gunner F/Sgt Walter Hurdle RNZAF. There was also extensive damage to the fuselage, the starboard flap was shot away and the port elevator almost severed. The pilot F/O E.F. Witting RNZAF was able to regain control and successfully flew the damaged aircraft back to base. F/O Witting is on the left of the group and F/Sgt Hurdle who was killed is 2nd from the right. Other members of the crew are Sgt R.E Morfett, M/U; Sgt A.R. Gunn, F/Eng; P/O J. Thomas, B/A; F/O W.E. Anderson, Nav; Sgt G. Marshall, W/Op.

Photograph taken at Harwell 1944 when 570 Squadron aircrew were receiving their emergency rations and escape kits prior to Ops. Extreme left arms folded: F/Sgt G. Wood, A/G; Next full face: McClelland Hope, F/Eng; Next arm to side: F/Sgt R.W.C. 'Happy' Hull, A/G; Full face with peak cap in centre: F/O Ron Spafford, Pilot; Receiving rations P/O W. Kirkham, Pilot; Over his shoulder: F/O D.H. Atkinson, B/A; Extreme right: F/O M. Hand, W/Op. Last three named all killed at Arnhem. P/O Kirkham took off at 1442 on 23rd September 1944 flying Stirling Mk.IV LJ883 V8-K. The aircraft was hit by flak over Arnhem DZ and crashed. The first named in the list F/Sgt Wood survived but all the other members of the crew including P/O E.C. Brown, Nav, and Sgt H. Ashton, F/Eng, were killed.

295 Squadron Rivenhall 1944. Mk.IV LJ591 8Z-J 'Just Jane' with air and ground crew. *Air crew back row L-R*: W/O Jock Esslemont, A/G; W/O Ron Durston, B/A; F/Lt Roy Scott, Pilot; F/Lt Douglas Burlington, Nav; F/Sgt John Rushforth, W/Op; F/Sgt Ray Mills, F/Eng. This aircraft completed nine Ops mainly SOE to France but after the war ended it also flew seventeen sorties carrying repatriated PoW's from Brussels, Gardermoen and Stavanger plus transported out food, clothing and stores to Prague and Copenhagen. Of the total sorties flown F/Lt Scott and his crew were responsible for sixteen of them.

Stirling Heavy Bomber Crew 199 Squadron, Lakenheath, November 1943. *L to R back row*: Sgt R.G. 'Mugsy' Knights, M/U; Sgt D. 'Duke' Oxley, F/Eng; Sgt W.R. Dunkley, R/G; Sgt A.C. Pool, W/Op. *Front*: Sgt L. Crossman, Nav; P/O Bill Chappell, Pilot; F/Sgt Tom Higgins, B/A. This crew were detailed to fly, among others, Stirling EF505, EF506, EF510, EF455, EF953 and EE910. They were all posted to 190 Squadron at the end of February 1944. F/Sgt Tom Higgins was in fact an American who came into the RAF via the Canadian Air Force and Sgt Knights went on to complete two tours.

Mk.V Stirling of Transport Command. The photograph was taken just after the war ended and shows the Stirling on display at one of the many air shows held around the country. There is quite a long line of people waiting to go inside the fuselage and inspect the interior.

Stirling Mk.V PJ958. This was the prototype of a civil conversion built by Short & Harland, Belfast and delivered to 23 Maintenance Unit on 4th April 1945. Returned to S&H for modifications 9th April 1945 and then spent time at the Air Transport Tactical Development Unit and Transport Command Development Unit undergoing further modifications and refinements. On 19th December 1945 when being flown into Harwell on route to TCDU at Brize Norton the aircraft touched down much too late – at least 400 yards further up the runway than normal. Consequently, running out of runway, the pilot F/Lt P.P. Mather turned sharply at the end onto the taxiway to avoid the bomb dump and the undercarriage collapsed. The airframe was written off as Cat E/FA but was subsequently brought back on charge on 17th January 1946, renumbered 5797M, and used for instructional purposes.